People to Know

Bill Gates
Billionaire Computer Genius

Joan D. Dickinson

Enslow Publishers, Inc.

40 Industrial Road	PO Box 38
Box 398	Aldershot
Berkeley Heights, NJ 07922	Hants GU12 6BP
USA	UK

http://www.enslow.com

Library of Congress Cataloging-in-Publication Data

Dickinson, Joan D.
    Bill Gates, billionaire computer genius / Joan D. Dickinson.
        p. cm. —(People to know)
    Includes bibliographical references and index.
    Summary: Presents a biography of the math whiz kid who grew up to co-found
Microsoft, the world's leading computer software firm.
    ISBN-10: 0-89490-824-3
    1. Gates, Bill, 1955- . —Juvenile literature. 2. Businessmen—United States—
Biography—Juvenile literature. 3. Computer software industry—United States—
History—Juvenile literature. 4. Microsoft Corporation—History—Juvenile
literature. [1. Gates, Bill, 1955- . 2. Businessmen. 3. Computer software industry.
4. Microsoft Corporation—History.] I. Title. II. Series.
HD9696.C62G334 1997
338.7'610053'092—dc21
    [B]   96-44529
                                                CIP
                                                AC
ISBN-13: 978-0-89490-824-8

Printed in the United States of America

10

Illustration Credits: Alan Berner/Seattle Times, pp. 11, 83; AP/Wide World
Photos, pp. 44, 58, 66, 73; Barry Wong/Seattle Times, pp. 33, 79; Charles
Loscalzo 1996, p. 28; Courtesy of Microsoft, pp. 4, 7, 52; Mike Siegel/Seattle
Times, p. 21; Newsday, Inc./Alan Raia, © 1994, p. 40; Newsday, Inc./Dick
Kraus, © 1996, p. 86; Newsday, Inc./Julia Gaines, © 1986, p. 88; Newsday,
Inc./Oliver Morris, © 1995, p. 62; Rich Andrews/Microsoft, p. 55; Teresa
Tamurn/Seattle Times, p. 70.

Cover Illustration: Courtesy of Microsoft

Contents

Bill Gates

The 18-Billion-Dollar Man

"I'd hate to be in business competition with Bill Gates, but as a consumer, it's hard not to like him."[1]

—Nick Sullivan, Senior Editor,
Home Office Computing

In the early 1970s, computer technology was just starting to grow. The programs were simple and rough. The computers themselves were often so large they filled the space of an entire room. They required constant air circulation for cooling and to prevent overheated circuits. The printers connected to these computers were slow, noisy, and bulky. Being very expensive, the computers were used primarily by large corporations, banks, and government agencies. These huge, awkward collections of metal and wire went through many design changes over the years. They eventually evolved into the desktop hardware versions we use today called the personal computer (PC).

Bill Gates is the cofounder, chairman, and chief executive officer (CEO) of Microsoft Corporation. He is the richest man in America. As of July 1996, his total current worth was approximately $18 billion.[2] He was only forty years old at that time. He built his vast fortune through his love for business and computers.

To fully understand how much money Bill Gates has accumulated, consider this: $18 billion is enough to pay the salary of the President of the United States for the next ninety thousand years.[3] With sincere devotion and a belief that the power of the computer should be available to everyone, Bill Gates became a multibillionaire.

In 1969, Bill Gates had a flash of what the future would hold for the new world of computers. While spending many hours in high school teaching himself about computers, he and his friend Paul Allen would talk about the unlimited possibilities. He asked Paul, "Don't you think that someday everybody will have one of these things? And if they did, couldn't you deliver magazines and newspapers and stuff through them? I mean, I wonder if you could make money doing something like that?"[4] Bill Gates was only thirteen at the time. Already he knew the computer was going to change his life.

In the years to come, Gates would be a leading force in creating a computer-driven society. With the help of his Microsoft products, almost any information anyone would need could be found easily.

Today, Microsoft's headquarters are in Redmond, Washington.

In January 1975, a microcomputer called the Altair 8800 appeared on the cover of *Popular Electronics* magazine. A couple of young, die-hard computer fans, Bill Gates and Paul Allen, were inspired by that article. As a result, they adapted an existing computer program called BASIC to use with the Altair 8800. It was the first language for the personal computer. Gates and Allen sold their version of BASIC to MITS, the maker of the Altair 8800. MITS, of Albuquerque, New Mexico, became the first customer of Gates and Allen's newly formed company, Microsoft. The computer revolution had started and Bill Gates was leading the charge.

Gates had long been called a whiz kid and a technical genius by many people. He firmly believed that computer technology would benefit many consumers and businesses. He knew computers could greatly enhance the quality and quantity of work done on them. Gates also felt advances in the technology would be very important. He dreamed that someday people would have access to more computing power for their everyday needs. He thought about using computers for paying bills, or listening to music, or browsing through an encyclopedia. Gates focused all his efforts on developing software to make such uses possible.

Gates knew that even the best hardware (the computer) was not worth much to people if they did not know how to use it. The hardware is the body of the computer, but the software is the brain. Gates knew he could write software to make the computer do what people wanted. His intense concentration and the courage to make his plan work put Microsoft at the top of the personal computer industry. By 1995, a Microsoft operating system could be found in 80 percent of the world's PCs.[5]

Gates is very loyal to the employees who work for him. He rewards his staff with promotions and stock options.[6] There are now an estimated three thousand employees who are "Microsoft Millionaires."[7] Microsoft has grown from a two-man operation into a multibillion-dollar computer powerhouse.[8]

Gates has had success with Microsoft for two reasons. First, he focused on designing software products that perform well and are easy to operate. Second, his stubborn pursuit of perfection pushed his Microsoft team to improve on their products. He believed in researching and investigating a software program until it was flawless.

Many of Microsoft's competitors worry that Gates may be too powerful.[9] He is known for having enormous ambition. Although he does not consider himself a good negotiator, he is good at getting what he needs for his company.[10]

Gates has great plans for new, innovative technology. He believes in the possibility of wireless wallet personal computers and computers that can handle natural language processing.[11] Gates feels Microsoft's software products "will be used in business, in the home, in the pocket and in the car."[12] The future looks very bright for the people at Microsoft, and for the man who will lead them there, Bill Gates.

The Gates
Family

Bill Gates was born into an extremely successful family. Both his maternal and paternal grandparents were wealthy and gifted self-starters. Gates's parents, William Henry Gates, Jr. (known as Bill Jr.), and Mary Maxwell Gates, were successful in their own right. Bill Jr. worked as a lawyer for the Seattle law firm of Skeel, McKelvy, Hanke, Everson & Uhlmann. Mary served on numerous corporate boards, including the United Way, the University of Washington, and First Interstate Bancorp.

Mary was a beautiful, outgoing girl. At school, her nickname was "Giggles." She grew up with some of the most important and famous families in the Pacific

Northwest. Bill Jr. was a reserved pre-law student when he met Mary on the University of Washington campus. They were married in 1952.

Bill and Mary were a very active couple. They attended many social and political gatherings. The Gateses had three children, Kristianne, William (Bill), and Elizabeth.

Bill Gates, born on October 28, 1955, grew up being called "Trey" by his family. Bill showed a sense of independence at a very early age. When his parents bought his first rocking horse, he immediately took to it, rocking back and forth for hours. "They used to put me to

Mary Gates, Bill's mother, was a prominent woman in her own right. She served on the boards of United Way, First Interstate Bancorp, and many other corporations.

sleep on my rocking horse and I think that addicted me."[1] Even as an adult, his rocking is famous in the halls at Microsoft. "He rocks at different levels of intensity according to his mood."[2]

As a boy, Bill Gates was skinny and small for his age. He had a high-pitched, squeaky voice and was left-handed. Gates was usually the youngest in his class at View Ridge Elementary School in Seattle. His birthday fell right before the November 1 cutoff for enrollment.

Even though he was smaller in size than his schoolmates, he had a very quick mind. He read the *World Book Encyclopedia* from A to Z by the time he was nine years old.[3] Gates was also very good at math. Other students would spend days learning multiplication tables, but Bill could recite them in an instant. He was so far ahead of the other students that he often became bored.

The Gates family spent much time playing card games. They enjoyed double solitaire, gin, and bridge. Bill's Grandma Adelle Maxwell, or "Gam" as he called her, taught Bill how to play. The Gateses loved competition. Rewards were given for winning and penalties were given for losing.[4]

The Gates family spent their summers swimming, diving, and sailing. In the winter, Bill was a fast and reckless snow skier. It was a sport where the player had to keep tight control yet be aggressive. It proved to be an indication of how his life would be. Pushing his power to the limits yet keeping focused was what Bill Gates was about.

School Days

Bill Gates started junior high school at the Lakeside School in 1967. It was an exclusive, all-boys private school. Gates went there for grades seven through twelve.

Lakeside was very different from his public grade school. There were strict rules for the students. The classes were very demanding, and the students were competitive. This was a good setting for the very smart boy, Bill, who got bored easily.

The atmosphere at Lakeside was very formal until the later 1960s. As students all over the country were protesting the war in Vietnam, so did the ones at Lakeside. Some of the rebellious attitude brought about great changes at the school. Soon students loosened up a bit. Their manner of dress became more casual. They traded in their suits for blue jeans, and grew their hair long. The world had changed and so did Lakeside.

When Bill started at Lakeside, he had a lot to learn. He was in a new school, with new rules and new friends. It was there that his aim for personal freedom developed. Bill became aware of ways to get noticed. Although Lakeside rewarded the boys who stayed in line and showed respect, Bill knew that the ones who stood out got more attention. They were given more support and encouragement by the teachers. Overall, the school allowed each student to find and develop his own interests. It was a place where Bill could apply his intense energy, competitive spirit, and business sense. In the years to come, he would realize that the opportunities offered at Lakeside changed his life forever.

Bill spent a great deal of time reading. The broad range of subjects he read helped him become very intelligent. While at Lakeside, "he went through a Napoleon phase, reading everything he could about the French conqueror."[1] On subjects he liked, Bill could absorb every detail. His high school English teacher recalls him memorizing a three-page soliloquy for a school play in one reading. He especially liked math and science.

Gates found a true friend named Kent Evans while at Lakeside. Evans, a minister's son, was also very skilled in math. The boys formed a close friendship based on their deep interest in computers. Bill became known as a math whiz kid. He and his friends were not very interested in sports or the arts or the many political and social changes of the 1960s. They were totally absorbed in the new technology.

In 1968, Bill Gates started the eighth grade. That year he had his first introduction to computers. Most mainframe computers were extremely expensive. They were purchased by banks or universities with large budgets. The Lakeside School instead invested in an affordable piece of office equipment that could communicate with a computer.

The ASR-33 Teletype machine was a noisy machine, usually found in newsrooms. It was a combination of a keyboard, printer, paper tape puncher, and modem. A modem can send signals through telephone lines. The ASR-33 used its modem to "talk" to an actual computer.

The computer itself was located in downtown Seattle. It was a PDP-10 (Program Data Processor) microcomputer that was much smaller than a mainframe, roughly the size of a refrigerator. It was one of the first small computers from Digital Equipment Corporation, also known as DEC.

One day Bill Gates's math teacher at Lakeside took his class to the computer room to see firsthand how the Teletype machine operated. Since Bill was such an outstanding math student, he was given the honor of typing a few instructions into the computer. With the help of his teacher, Bill sent the commands through the modem to the waiting PDP-10. Everyone was amazed a few moments later when the Teletype machine printed its clickety-clack response.[2]

For the students at Lakeside, communication with

computers was now possible, and a whole new world was opening. Lakeside was one of the first schools in the country to have the use of a computer. The students were offered a glimpse into the future.

Lakeside did not offer computer courses, but Bill and his friends decided to learn all they could about the machine. Soon they knew more about computers than any teacher or adult at the school.[3]

A usage fee was charged every time the Teletype machine communicated with the Seattle PDP-10 computer. Even though Lakeside had a budget for the new equipment, they still needed to keep the expenses within reason. They decided to charge a fee to students who used the Teletype.

The parents of the Lakeside students were just as excited about the Teletype as the students, so a group of mothers, called the Lakeside Mothers Club, decided to help out with the cost of the computer time. They held a rummage sale and donated the proceeds.[4] The Mothers Club expected the money to pay for a year's worth of computer time. They did not realize, though, that the boys were spending every moment possible in the computer room. The money was all used up in just a few short weeks!

The computer room was the place to be to learn the new technology. Gates was quickly drawn in by the many possible functions the computer could perform. He read everything relating to computers that he could get his hands on. Bill often taught himself as he went along. He learned by trial and error. Since the teachers did not have any real working knowledge of computers, they usually let the students "play" alone in the computer room.

Soon Bill was able to write computer programs to use through the Teletype machine. Among his first was a tic-tac-toe game.[5] It was basically a series of instructions telling the computer where to make the next move. He used a computer language known as BASIC (Beginner's All-Purpose Symbolic Instruction Code). It had been developed in 1964 by two professors from Dartmouth College. BASIC was very interesting to the young programmer because it was based in math. It used two binary numbers, zero and one, to talk to the computer.

Another big computer fan was also constantly in the computer room. Paul Allen, a tenth grader known for being soft-spoken and friendly, was two years older than Bill. Paul spent much of his time reading and had a large collection of science-fiction novels. He was raised in a family of readers and thinkers. Paul's father, Kenneth Allen, was an associate director of libraries for the University of Washington.

Paul and Bill spent much of their time talking about the future of computer technology. They quickly realized there was no limit to the possibilities. Paul was interested in the hardware, where Bill focused on the power of software.

The two boys joined two other friends, Richard Weiland and Kent Evans, to form the Lakeside Programmers Group. Their goal was to find ways to make money in the business world using the computer. Bill Gates had been preparing himself for this opportunity by reading many business magazines.

The average grade school student did not spend time reading about business, but Bill was far from average.

Bill was actually thrown out of the group at one point, but his friends soon realized they needed his shrewd business sense. Bill came back to the Lakeside Programmers Group and before long became its president.[6]

It became very obvious that Bill's intensity and competitiveness in business was fierce. It was an attitude that he would bring in adulthood to Microsoft and that is very well known in the industry. When it came to business, not even friendship would stand in his way.

As the power of computing was reaching the business world, new, related businesses were opening. One was a company called Computer Center Corporation, which was fondly known as C-Cubed. C-Cubed had a great idea for their business. First the management obtained a DEC computer. Then C-Cubed tried to make a fortune by selling time to users of its computer. In the busy Seattle area, many businesses such as accounting firms and engineering firms could benefit from using computers. C-Cubed saw potential business in all these companies.[7]

One of the founders of C-Cubed had a son who was also a student at Lakeside. He told her about the intense programmers who hung around the computer room. She offered these students free computer time in exchange for testing new software. The boys' job was to report any "bugs," or glitches, in the software.

The boys accepted the offer. They soon spent every Saturday and added more time after school as well.

Bill became very skilled at finding bugs—often crashing, or stopping, the computer system. He quickly understood the power of the software. Without software that was easy to operate, the hardware was useless. Bill became totally obsessed with programming. He skipped many gym classes to get back to the computers.[8]

As he became so focused on writing programming codes for software, he began to overlook the simple things of everyday life. His appearance became sloppy and unkempt. The floor of his bedroom was littered with dirty laundry and rolls of computer paper.

In March of 1970, Computer Center Corporation closed its business. The engineers and creative people who started the company never actually broke into the computer leasing business as they had planned. For the boys at Lakeside, it proved to be a good example of how life in the business world worked.

By 1971, Bill, Paul, and a few friends had started a company called Traf-O-Data. Paul was now a freshman at Washington State University. Bill was still at Lakeside.

Traf-O-Data was a service designed to read the data that municipalities collected to show traffic patterns. The information came from a rubber hose that was placed across a road.

Each time a car crossed it, a computer punched its time onto a tape, using the binary numbers zero and one. The data were used to determine the timing for traffic lights and to see if roadwork was necessary. The boys realized they could provide the service faster and cheaper than the private companies hired to read the data.[9]

In a short while, the boys saw the need to create their own computer to analyze the traffic-counter tape directly. They hired an engineer to help build the hardware they needed. With $360, Bill and Paul bought an Intel 8008 microprocessor chip to be the brain.[10] Now they had a computer. They could feed the tapes directly into their computer to analyze the data.

Traf-O-Data would later fold when Bill left for college in 1973. The company never achieved real success, but it did prove to be a valuable experience. The entrepreneur had his first real crack at funding and running a business. Both he and Paul learned that computers had great potential for making money.

In 1972, Bill Gates was chosen to be a summer congressional page in Washington, D.C. His job required doing a lot of "grunt work" that no one else wanted to do, such as running errands. During his stay, he managed to find a great business opportunity. This story has taken on a legendary quality over the years.

When Senator George McGovern was making his bid for the presidency in 1972, his vice president of choice was Senator Thomas Eagleton of Missouri. A scandal soon broke: Eagleton had been undergoing psychiatric care and electroshock therapy for depression. Would the public vote for a candidate being treated for depression? With a major election at stake, a chance like this could not be taken. The proposed

Bill Gates and Paul Allen became close friends in junior high at Lakeside School. They shared an interest in computers—and in making money. Gates and Allen started their first computer business, Traf-o-Data, a few years later.

partnership did not last. Eagleton was dropped off the ticket. Realizing that the campaign buttons reading "McGovern/Eagleton" were no longer useful, Bill conjured up a plan. As the story goes, he bought up thousands of campaign buttons and later resold them for a large profit as collector's items.[11]

In the middle of his senior year at Lakeside, Bill got permission from his parents and the school to take time off from school and accept an offer for full-time work. The company was TRW, a huge government defense contractor. TRW needed the best programmers they could find to help out with some urgent projects. They hired Paul Allen and Bill Gates. Bill was paid about $4.10 an hour, which was a little more than minimum wage.

The experience at TRW gave Bill a chance to perfect his programming skills. He found a mentor in John Norton, a top-notch programmer at TRW. Norton always commented on a programmer's code, and Gates liked that.

Today at Microsoft, Bill is known for sending electronic mail, or E-mail, to his programmers with his comments. His notes are often critical. More than once programmers have received E-mail from Bill Gates that started, "This is the stupidest piece of code ever written."[12]

The Birth of Microsoft

Bill Gates returned to Lakeside during the second half of his senior year. After graduation, he entered Harvard University in Cambridge, Massachusetts. It was 1973, and Gates was not quite eighteen.

For Bill, life at Harvard was vastly different from his days at Lakeside. The school was known for attracting the best and brightest students from around the world. Bill enrolled in the most difficult freshman math course he could. He had always had a deep passion for math and a keen ability to see a shortcut to solve any mathematics problem.[1] He had scored a perfect 800 on his math SAT (Scholastic Aptitude Test).[2] At one point, he thought of becoming a math professor—"until he met other students who were better at math than he was."[3] Bill was no longer the top student of the class. He had spent many years feeling the power of being the brightest student at Lakeside, but at Harvard he was just another smart guy.

Bill spent most of his time at Harvard playing pinball, staying up for all-night poker games, and programming.[4] With a near-photographic memory, he was able to pass classes with little effort, but his grades were not the best they could be. He spent a lot of time at Aiken Hall, the computer center on campus. The more he worked with the software, the more convinced he was it would become his life's work.

This put Gates in a serious dilemma. He knew his dreams of making money with computers could be realized, but not while studying at Harvard. He and Paul Allen had often discussed the idea of forming their own software company. They spoke of how they would run their business. On the other side, Bill's parents wanted their son to continue his studies. They talked of his possibly becoming a lawyer, following in his father's footsteps. Gates had other ideas in mind. He knew he had a passion for computers, but was not sure how it would be a career. Then one day in early 1975, something happened that set Gates's career wheels in motion.

While walking in Harvard Square, Paul Allen saw a magazine that caught his eye. The cover of the January 1975 issue of *Popular Electronics* showed a photo of a computer, the MITS Altair 8800. Under that, the cover read, "the world's first minicomputer kit to rival commercial models."[5] It was the first microcomputer available to electronics fans at an affordable price. "Look!" Allen said, as he rushed to show Gates the article. "It's going to happen! . . . And we're going to miss it."[6] The two computer fanatics quickly read about the new hardware.

The Altair 8800 was a box with a series of toggle switches and lights on the front. There was no monitor or keyboard. It was manufactured by MITS, Micro Instrumentation and Telemetry Systems, of Albuquerque, New Mexico. MITS, owned by Ed Roberts, was a successful electronics company that made money in commercial calculators. In the early 1970s, competition became fierce in the calculator market. By 1974, MITS was deep in debt. Roberts knew he was in trouble. He decided to market a new microprocessor with the Intel 8080 chip to computer fans. The name Altair came from an episode of *Star Trek* in which the starship *Enterprise* was headed to the star Altair.[7] The term "personal computer" came out of the advertising campaign for the Altair 8800. "I was trying to convey a small machine you could afford to buy that didn't sound like a toy," Roberts said.[8]

Roberts was very interested in the possible functions of computers. He had built the Altair because he wanted to play with one himself. He decided to sell the kits to other hobbyists who might be looking to do the same.

The article in *Popular Electronics* proved a huge success. Computer enthusiasts across the country began ordering the Altair. Roberts had hoped to sell a few hundred of the kits. Even he was surprised when he had a backlog of thousands of orders.[9] Hobbyists everywhere wanted their own PCs to play with.

The Altair 8800 kit came with a few problems. It was very difficult to assemble, even for the best electronics wizards. Once it was together, it was virtually useless. For $397, the computer hobbyist who successfully constructed the kit had nothing more than a piece of hardware with blinking lights when he was done. The kit did not include a keyboard or a screen. In addition, no software yet existed that would make it work. The two young computer fans, Gates and Allen, saw an opportunity to make something useful out of the Altair.[10]

They quickly saw that a language was needed to communicate with the Altair. Gates and Allen wanted to create the first software for the Altair. "We realized that the revolution might happen without us. After that article, there was no question of where our life would focus," said Gates.[11]

The 8080 was a much more powerful processor than the 8008 processor in the Lakeside computer. Allen and Gates figured an adapted version of BASIC would have the best chance for success on the Altair. BASIC, used for large computers, was considered a simple language, easy to use and learn. It would be a good match for the young computer hobbyists across the country who wanted their own computer. Gates and Allen contacted Ed Roberts and told him they had already written a version of BASIC to run on his computer. In truth, they had not actually written anything yet, but they knew they had to move fast. (In the years to come, the announcing of products that don't exist would become standard at Bill Gates's Microsoft Corporation. This strategy is known in the industry as "vaporware." The idea is to discourage the competition from developing a product by announcing that you made it first.)

Ed Roberts was interested in the BASIC program for his Altair. He wanted to see their software. Gates and Allen went quickly to work. They went on an eight-week writing binge. Gates wrote most of the computer code, ". . . often falling asleep at the keyboard, dreaming in code, waking up, and immediately starting to write code again . . ."[12] They were working around the clock to meet the challenge. Gates spent day and night at the Aiken Computer Center at Harvard. He started skipping classes, knowing his deadline was looming.

Allen and Gates did not have an Altair to test their software on. "We just had this book that described the machine. If we had read the book wrong, or the book was wrong, we were hosed," said Gates.[13] Allen wrote a computer program that made the PDP-10 computer at Harvard mimic the 8080 chip. It was a very difficult task, but he was successful. This enabled them to keep working as though they had an Altair. They used their skills to write a program tight, or small, enough to fit the Altair computer's limited memory.[14]

The team of Gates and Allen contacted Ed Roberts and arranged for a meeting at the MITS office. Allen had the honor of flying to MITS for the presentation. He was chosen because he looked more mature than Gates. It was a tense time for Allen. He knew he would

While he was a student at Harvard, Gates spent much of his time at Aiken Hall in the computer room. There he decided that creating software would be his life's work.

make a fool of himself if the program did not work. It would take only one bug to crash the program. With the first BASIC code written for a microcomputer in hand, Allen went to Albuquerque, New Mexico.

At the MITS office, Allen set up the paper tape with the BASIC code to be read by the Altair 8800. He entered the "bootstrap," a program that instructed the computer how to load BASIC. As he sat in the meeting with Ed Roberts, Allen knew this was their moment of truth. Many hours of hard work and dreams came down to this one instant. The Altair was now ready. Allen asked it to add 2 + 2. He silently held his breath. He tried not to show his surprise when it printed back 4. Gates and Allen's BASIC program was a success![15] "One little mistake would have meant the program wouldn't have run. The first time we tried it was at MITS, and it came home without a glitch," said Gates.[16]

With the BASIC program, the chunky metal box was transformed into a working computer. The Altair could now have a real use. Back in Massachusetts, Gates and Allen toasted their victory with ice cream and soft drinks. Their lives had been changed forever.

Allen worked closely with the MITS staff. They needed him to work out any possible problems. In March 1975, he was offered a job at MITS as software director. Things were looking up.

Gates and Allen discussed an exclusive licensing agreement with MITS. The two programmers realized that a major market for software was being born, and they wanted to cash in on their hard work. Although Gates was still a student at Harvard and Allen was working for MITS, they knew it was time for them to form their own company.

After his second year at Harvard ended, Bill Gates joined Allen in Albuquerque for the summer. Their new company, Microsoft, was officially set up in business as a partnership. The name is a combination of "microcomputer" and "software."

Bill Gates was only nineteen years old at the time. With help from his father and an attorney, the MITS licensing contract was written. Gates's agreement provided for licensing royalties of BASIC whether or not it was sold with a MITS computer kit. This opened a new world for the licensing of software. In the earliest days of the personal computer, software was written by the user of the computer and shared among friends. Microsoft's contract with MITS set the stage for future legal cases over software piracy.

In February 1976, Gates became one of the first programmers to raise the software piracy issue. In *Computer Notes*, the MITS Altair newsletter, Gates wrote a sharp letter accusing some computer hobbyists of stealing software. He was convinced that the sales of their BASIC software should have been higher. He believed the reason sales were lower was that people illegally copied the software. In his letter, "An Open Letter to Hobbyists," Gates said the piracy of software prevented the development of good programs.[17] He added that people who copy and resell BASIC give all hobbyists a bad name.

In March 1976, Gates gave the opening address at the First Annual World Altair Computer Convention in Albuquerque. Anyone and everyone who was remotely connected to the Altair came to the convention. They were eager to test the new technology.

In the end of 1976, Paul Allen left his position at MITS. He joined Microsoft full time.

At the start of 1977, Bill Gates dropped out of Harvard University and never looked back. He was positive the software business he and Paul Allen planned would be worth more than any college degree. Now both men were able to put all their time, energy, and attention into Microsoft plans.

At Microsoft, the new partners fit into a balanced working relationship. Gates spent most of his time negotiating with the computer manufacturers. Although he was young, he had a tremendous understanding of complex technology. He appreciated the legal issues surrounding software. Allen focused on programming and creating new technology.

Gates spent many hours pitching new contracts. One big-name business he landed a deal with was the Tandy Corporation in Fort Worth, Texas. Tandy had opened in 1927 as a leather business. It moved into the blazing electronics market in 1962 when it purchased a nine-store chain called Radio Shack. Over the next decade, hundreds of Radio Shack stores opened across the country. In Texas, Tandy was known as the "McDonald's of the electronics world."[18] Their TRS-80 computer came off the assembly line ready to use. Gates wanted the TRS-80 to be equipped with his software.

Tandy licensed Gates and Allen's version of BASIC in 1977. The match was received with an enthusiastic ring of cash registers from consumers.

There were other players in the electronics game Gates wanted to pursue. In 1977 Gates made a licensing agreement with Apple Computer for Microsoft's BASIC 6502. This version of BASIC was designed for the Apple II computers. Shortly after closing that deal, Gates began making aggressive calls to the Japanese market. He wanted to let the competition know he was preparing to sell his software worldwide.

In November 1977, MITS lost its exclusive licensing deal for BASIC after a long battle over royalty and distribution rights. A dispute over how to promote the Altair and BASIC divided the partnership. MITS fell into financial trouble and closed.

By the end of 1977, the partners were discussing moving their business. It was growing rapidly. Albuquerque was too difficult to get to and no longer an ideal location. Allen wanted to return to Seattle. They also talked about Silicon Valley in California, where other computer businesses were based. Gates's main concerns were potential for expanding the business and easy access to the office for him, his staff, and clients. He agreed to Seattle.

At Microsoft, Gates's push for global offices was working. In June 1978, Gates and Allen opened Microsoft Far East in Japan. Other office locations around the world soon followed. Gates's business savvy would pay off. Today, 58 percent of Microsoft's total revenue comes from international markets.[19]

Life at Microsoft was not always smooth. Sometimes the amount of time needed for a project would be greatly underestimated. Deadlines were

In the early days of Microsoft, Gates negotiated deals with computer manufacturers while Allen concentrated on programming and creating new technology. Here the partners discuss product strategies.

missed. The products that were shipped were not always designed as well as they could have been. Gates wanted his new software products out quickly just so they could be the first on the market. He did not like to waste time. His programmers kept fine-tuning the products even after their release.

Society was being empowered by the use of computers. Bill Gates wanted Microsoft software to be used on each and every one sold. Microsoft was setting the standard in personal computers.

On January 1, 1979, two major events took place in the history of Microsoft. The company officially moved to Bellevue, Washington, and BASIC 5.0 was released. Gates and Allen's version of BASIC was now in literally every PC available.[20]

MS-DOS and IBM

Business at Microsoft was rapidly expanding, and it demanded more attention from Bill Gates. The computer industry was gaining strength. Suddenly more and more companies wanted to cash in on the business.

In 1979, the Intel company introduced a new microprocessor chip—the 8086 chip. It was specifically designed for use in personal computers. The 8080 had been the industry standard, and many programs relied on the chip to run. A computer reads (processes) one word at a time, but the "words" can be different lengths. The 8080 used an 8-bit "word." The 8086's words were twice as long—16 bits. This means the 8086 was dramatically faster. Although many in the industry believed the new chip would not replace the 8080, Gates and Allen thought differently. The two decided to build their own computer system. Microsoft began work on a version of BASIC software to work with the 8086 hardware. They needed an operating system, the program that runs the computer, to make it work.

Tim Paterson, a computer engineer, had built a computer that worked with the 8086 processor chip. He worked for a small company called Seattle Computer Products, which was owned by Rod Brock. The company built memory boards for microcomputers. Paterson convinced Brock that Seattle Computer Products should design a central processing unit, or CPU, to run with Intel's new 8086 chip. Paterson knew that Microsoft was working on an 8086 BASIC. In May 1979, Paterson offered his computer prototype to Microscoft to run their software. In June, Microsoft's new BASIC software, running on Seattle Computer's new CPU, was presented at the annual National Computer Conference in New York City.

By late 1979, Seattle Computers was marketing its new CPU. Seattle had planned to use CP/M (Control Program for Microcomputers), an operating system that a company called Digital Research was working on, but Digital missed its scheduled delivery date. Paterson felt Seattle Computer was losing sales because of the delay. He needed an operating system. He decided to take action and develop one himself. It was intended as a temporary fix for the waiting customers. In five months, Paterson's new operating system for the 16-bit hardware was ready to run. Paterson called it 86-QDOS, for "quick and dirty operating system." Paterson's 86-QDOS loosely mirrored CP/M, but also had improvements.

Other companies were making progress in the computer world, too. One was Apple Computer. Based on a partnership between Steve Jobs and Steve Wozniak, Apple had begun in a garage in Cupertino, California. The partners belonged to a unique group of driven geniuses called the Homebrew Computer Club. The club was a place where serious computer fans could exchange ideas. It was there that Steve Wozniak had brought the early Apple computer to impress his friends. Steve Jobs saw great business potential in the Apple.[1] They formed a partnership based on Jobs's vision for the Apple's future.

Gates heard about their work with a new microprocessor called the 6502. Microsoft offered to sell BASIC to Apple, but Apple declined. Jobs and Wozniak believed they could write their own program, one that was easier to use. A quick glance into the future would prove them correct.

Bill Gates found a way into the Apple Computer market. In August 1980, Microsoft released a software/hardware enhancement called the SoftCard. It was the brainchild of Paul Allen. The SoftCard allowed the owners of Apple II computers to run CP/M applications. Apple had taken many steps to protect its products from being "cloned," or copied. Apple computers were produced with a unique chip, the 6502, and had their own operating system. Prior to the SoftCard's debut, only Apple software could run on an Apple computer. But now, by simply plugging Microsoft's SoftCard into the computer, a user could make the Apple ready to run any programs written for CP/M. Allen's idea was quickly accepted among Apple users and was highly profitable for Microsoft. In its first two years, more than sixty thousand SoftCards were sold.[2]

Computer technology was drastically changing. It was becoming very difficult to stay on the cutting edge. The needs and demands of computer users were quickly changing, too. In the earlier days, programmers were hired to write specific programs for a particular company. The software was tailor-made for the client's hardware and specific needs.

Soon many companies were in need of similar programs. Software for everyday business tasks such as word processing and accounting was in demand. Bill Gates saw an opportunity that he had not before considered. What if Microsoft created products that businesses could simply buy off the shelf? Potential customers could number in the thousands, or possibly millions. According to Gates, "the original insight for Microsoft was this: What if computing was free? The answer: Individuals would use computers as a tool, and software standards would become critical elements in making this happen."[3] Software could be a hot commodity where prices rose with demand. Microsoft now had another focus.

In July 1980, International Business Machines, or IBM, approached Gates for a project. They wanted Microsoft to write an operating system for a secret microcomputer they had in development. IBM also needed a language for its personal computer and was very interested in BASIC.

IBM was aware of the potential fortune in mass-marketed personal computers. This was a major departure for IBM. Its focus had been on mainframe systems, a highly profitable business. In the early 1980s, its revenue was approaching $30 billion a year. Management had previously thought the low-end microcomputers were not worth the effort. A closer look at the promising future of computers encouraged a change in direction. Not wanting to lag behind, the company needed to get products to the store shelves quickly.

IBM decided to use an outside source to save time and headaches. This was a very unusual move for IBM, also known as "Big Blue." (It earned the nick-name because company executives there all wore dark blue suits and starched white shirts as their "uniform.") Disclosing internal company documents to an outsider was unheard of, but IBM wanted to move quickly. They decided they would build their computers using pieces from other computer-parts manufacturers. The upstart company called Microsoft caught their eye.

In the meeting with IBM, Microsoft was asked to sign a nondisclosure document. The document was a legal agreement stating the people involved in the project could not discuss it with anyone else. The discussions of the day were top secret, and IBM was protecting itself.

First of all, IBM would need an operating system for its new computers. Microsoft did not have an

The IBM building in New York City. IBM enlisted Gates and his Microsoft team for a top-secret project—the pioneering IBM Personal Computer.

operating system to suit IBM's needs, so Gates suggested that IBM contact Digital Research, located in Pacific Grove, California. Gary Kidall, the owner, had developed the original CP/M, the most popular operating system in the computer industry at the time. Gates called Kidall and made arrangements for a meeting with IBM for the next day. That meeting, though, never took place.

More than one explanation of the events of the next day has been whispered and rumored. One scenario says that Gary Kidall purposely stood up the IBM executives. Another possibility says that Kidall and the Digital Research Company did not want to sign the nondisclosure agreement. Kidall has hinted over the years that he was not necessarily thrilled at the prospect of doing business with the "suits." IBM represented many things programmers did not like about the way the computer industry ran. Regardless of the reason, IBM's trip to California to find an operating system was in vain. Digital Research did not reach an agreement to sell CP/M to IBM. IBM turned back to Bill Gates for help.

IBM asked Microsoft to come up with an operating system, as well as the BASIC software, for the new secret microcomputers. On the surface it sounded like a great project. Gates knew the power IBM held in the marketplace. A business linked to IBM was almost guaranteed success. This partnership would propel Microsoft into an elite level of businesses. However, there was one problem Gates had to consider. The project was due in less than one year, a very tight deadline.

Completion of this assignment meant much more to Microsoft than just finishing another project and making money. Gates knew that without an operating system, the whole IBM PC plan would fall apart. IBM was staking its business and reputation on Microsoft. Microsoft was on the brink of success, if only it could get the job done. In addition to the extremely tight time frame, there was the huge financial commitment to consider. Could they spend the time and money needed to develop an operating system and meet the deadline? Then Allen thought of the answer to their operating system problem: Another system already existed and might be available for purchase. Microsoft called Seattle Computer Products.

Seattle Computer was told that Microsoft had a potential customer for Seattle's 86-QDOS. Gates chose not to say who the client was. He knew Microsoft could very easily be eliminated from the deal if Seattle Computer went directly to IBM. With his characteristic shrewdness and business smarts, Gates proved to be a genius at playing in the big leagues.

Seattle Computer signed a licensing agreement with Microsoft. The contract gave Microsoft nonexclusive rights to market the operating system. One clause in the agreement stated, "Nothing in this licensing agreement shall require Microsoft to identify its customer to Seattle Computer Products."[4] Although this secrecy struck him as odd, Rod Brock agreed to the terms. He had no way of knowing that Microsoft's client was one of the most powerful and wealthy companies in the world.

With an operating system lined up, Microsoft was ready to finalize the deal with IBM.

Paul Allen, Bill Gates, and a key manager, Kuzuhiko (Kay) Nishi, got together to discuss a strategy. Gates contacted IBM, proposal prepared.

A meeting was arranged between the legal department at IBM and the aggressive team at Microsoft. Gates and a few key Microsoft managers flew down to Florida to meet with the IBM executives. On the plane, Gates realized he had forgotten to pack a tie. They immediately drove around town to find one before the meeting. Although usually dressed very casually, Gates knew the importance of this meeting. He knew he had to "dress the part" to be taken seriously. As it was, some of the executives at Big Blue were a little surprised to see their future partner was so young. Even in a suit, Gates looked just like all the other hackers they had heard about.[5]

The Microsoft team and the IBM executives carefully reviewed all the technical and financial details of the deal. One of the points was a royalty arrangement. At that time, management at IBM had not really considered the potential windfall of profits in the sales of software. Their focus was on hardware, and their new secret line of computers. IBM agreed from the beginning that Microsoft would retain ownership rights to any software developed for IBM. Gates would have it no other way.

The meeting was long and draining for both sides, but successful. Rocking back and forth in his distinctive way, Gates answered a battery of questions with authority and confidence. He appeared much wiser

Bill Gates, who in 1980 forgot to pack a tie for his big meeting with IBM, has learned to "dress the part" for speaking engagements today.

than a twenty-four-year-old. He had a chance to spend time talking to Don Estridge, the team leader for Project Chess. This was the code name IBM had given to the project. Estridge was twenty years his senior, but the two shared a very strong common bond—their passion for computers.

In November 1980, IBM and Microsoft officially became business partners. IBM agreed to supply Microsoft with models of its new, secret line of personal computers. Microsoft agreed to develop the critical operating system and software. The race had begun.

Soon IBM had two prototypes of the small, desktop computer stored at Microsoft. IBM installed strict security measures to ensure the secrecy of its investment. Frequent surprise visits and spot checks were made to the Microsoft building in Seattle to guarantee the project was secure.

The staff at Microsoft, or "Microsofties" as they were known to others in the industry, worked day and night on the IBM project. For one solid year, the programmers and managers spent every waking moment focused on the project. They were sworn to secrecy and knew the importance of their mission. It was a game of beat the clock; every minute counted.

Seattle Computer's operating system was used as a basis for one of the most profitable products Microsoft ever developed, MS-DOS. In January 1981, Seattle Computer sold Microsoft the exclusive license to market 86-QDOS. The price was $50,000.[6]

On August 12, 1981, IBM introduced its Personal Computer with MS-DOS to the mass market.

Gates Becomes a Millionaire

During the 1980s, Microsoft benefited from explosive growth in the computer market. The company was quickly evolving, and there were many personnel changes. New products were being hastily introduced into the marketplace. The computer industry was growing up. Computer capabilities had gone beyond what even the wildest science-fiction fan could imagine. Technology was changing the way companies conducted their businesses and the way consumers organized their lives.

Microsoft was emerging as a dynamo in the industry. Microsoft's deal with IBM blasted Microsoft into the nobility of the business world. Their association with the mighty IBM helped make MS-DOS a world standard. Royalties from that one program were estimated at $200 million a year for several years.[1] IBM grossly underestimated the drive and stamina of Bill Gates. IBM's agreement to give Microsoft royalties for every IBM PC sold with MS-DOS proved to be a very costly mistake. The deal also allowed Microsoft to license MS-DOS to other computer manufacturers besides IBM. At that time, many other companies were building their own machines. They made and sold the hardware for less money than IBM did. When Japanese "clones" streamed into the United States computer markets, many had MS-DOS installed. Microsoft profited by receiving royalties on every one of those imported computers.

Paul Allen was an invaluable resource to Microsoft. Although he was very ambitious and a programming genius, his attitude was not as rough as Gates's. He was driven to master the project at hand, but had a social life outside the office as well. Allen enjoyed watching the Seattle SuperSonics play basketball, and played electric guitar in a local band. He was an integral part of building the Microsoft empire. Then, something happened that changed his whole life.

In 1982, Allen was diagnosed with Hodgkin's disease, a cancer of the lymph nodes. Allen was able to beat the disease with radiation therapy, but he came away with a new outlook on life. "You realize life is short. Facing your own mortality forces you to reevaluate your priorities."[2] Allen resigned from Microsoft in February 1983. He kept his shares of the company stock. A few years later Allen would return to Microsoft's board of directors.

In the 1980s Microsoft raced to the market with the hottest products it could develop. The other major players in the industry were making great strides, too. One in particular made Gates stop and take notice. It was Apple Computer.

Steve Jobs and Steve Wozniak developed a unique operating system called a graphic user interface, or GUI (pronounced "gooey"). With a small, handheld device, the user simply pointed and clicked on an icon, or picture, to perform a task. The technology was originally created by the Xerox Corporation at its Palo Alto Research Center (PARC) many years before. Xerox had not developed it for commercial use. The team at Apple made some changes to suit their needs. They intended to use the GUI with their new secret computer, the Macintosh.

Gates arranged a meeting with his friend Steve Jobs in 1982. They agreed Microsoft would develop programs for the new line of Apple computers. In October 1984, Microsoft introduced File and Word for Macintosh. They quickly became among the most popular software programs for the Macintosh.

With a GUI, operating a computer was very easy. The user was given a menu of choices across the top of the screen. Then a simple click on an icon would open up a program. The GUI was sold exclusively by Apple for its computers. All the IBM PCs and clones ran with MS-DOS.

Bill Gates saw the GUI at work. He had great ideas for applications using this new interface for DOS. He envisioned a system where text and graphics could be used together. He wanted features that could create an electronic office where items that appeared in a real office could be found on the screen. The system would have icons, menus, a file cabinet, and a wastebasket. By using the GUI, the user could open several programs at once. The system, Gates thought, should also be able to print a document in the same format as seen on the screen.

What started as a stroke of inspiration would take two years to complete. In 1981, Microsoft began development of one of its most successful software programs—Windows. With Windows, the user could open up more than one program at a time. Before Windows, the user had to close each project before another could be opened.

Other software companies were developing GUI programs as well. Gates wanted Microsoft products to be the industry standard. That meant his programmers would have to work faster. Gates also needed the support of other software developers. He used his tact and undying enthusiasm to sell them his idea of computing with the GUI. Gates formed a team of over twenty computer makers who agreed to support Windows. They included a wide assortment of companies, including Compaq, Hewlett-Packard, and Digital Equipment Corporation (DEC). IBM was the one major player obviously missing from the group. IBM was developing its own GUI, called TopView. The smaller companies rallied around Microsoft. They did not want to give IBM an opportunity to shut them out by setting the standard.

In April 1983, Microsoft introduced an inexpensive handheld peripheral (attachment to a computer system) called the Microsoft Mouse. The Mouse operated a pointer on screen to tell the computer which program to open. In the next eight years, over 6 million units of the Mouse would be sold worldwide.[3]

The Windows team worked at a frantic pace. In September 1983, Microsoft created Word for MS-DOS. It was a full-featured word processing program. Microsoft introduced the program with a demonstration disk included in the October issue of *PC World*. Ten years later, Word was the most popular word processing program in the world.[4]

The management at Apple had its own great dreams for computing success. The Macintosh, named after Steve Jobs's favorite fruit, made its memorable debut in January 1984 on a television ad that ran only once. The millions of viewers who watched the Oakland Raiders beat the Washington Redskins in Super Bowl XVII were treated to a unique commercial: A roomful of people who looked like zombies, drearily dressed, stared at a huge screen, where "Big Brother" droned on and on. Suddenly, a woman wearing bright clothes burst into the room. She heaved a sledgehammer at the screen and it shattered to pieces. The clever tagline then appeared on the screen: "On January 24, Apple Computer will introduce the Macintosh. And you'll see why 1984 won't be like 1984."[5] The reference was to George Orwell's famous novel *1984*, and the message was clear. Apple was not going to let IBM control and dominate the entire computing industry.

Microsoft expanded and matured as quickly as the market was moving. In August 1985, Microsoft celebrated its tenth anniversary. It had over one thousand employees. Company sales reached $140 million.[6] More space was needed. That summer, construction crews broke ground for a new corporate headquarters. On February 26, 1986, Microsoft moved to its new site in Redmond, Washington. The site is called the Corporate Campus.

The Campus was built on 270 wooded acres. There are 26 buildings equaling 4.1 million square feet of office space.[7] All the buildings are situated around a pond. The grounds provide a great setting for strolling or playing softball.

Life at the Campus is fast and furious. Currently, the average age of a Microsoftie is about thirty-four. Two-thirds of the employees are male.[8] The dress code is casual, mostly jeans and T-shirts. Ties are usually reserved only for top management meetings that are held off the Campus. The corporate culture is friendly and spirited.

The employees work very hard. Bill Gates demands dedication and loyalty from his team. He motivates his dynamic programmers to work up to eighty hours a week. He believes they should work just as hard as he does for the company. When they finally do take a break, the Microsofties have been known to play pranks on each other and management. They even have a special room just for juggling.

They communicate primarily through electronic mail (E-mail). Everyone in the company addresses Gates as "Bill." He nurtures an atmosphere at the

Microsoft built its headquarters, called the Corporate Campus, on 270 wooded acres in Redmond, Washington. The 26 buildings total 4.1 million square feet of office space.

Campus that encourages creative thinking. Gates believes in giving his employees an opportunity to develop to their fullest potential.

In his effort to be the leader in computer innovation, Gates created several different service units. Each group targets specific customers' needs, whether they are a business, manufacturer, or end user. (An end user is an individual person using a computer.)

Gates was leading the world into an electronic society. With awe and great anticipation, the world followed. Gates and several key executives decided it was time to take Microsoft to the next level of business. On March 13, 1986, Microsoft went public. This meant that shares of the company would be available for purchase to people outside the company. Selling shares would help Gates raise money to expand the company. Gates had been giving shares of stock in the company to employees as a benefit to attract the brightest and most talented people. The young, eager employees saw potential fortunes in owning the stock. Microsoft was a very healthy company. The business had available cash and no debt. All its growth had been funded internally.

On the open market, the stock was offered at $21 per share. By the closing bell on Wall Street for that day, the stock was trading at $28 per share. This initial public offering raised $61 million for Microsoft.[9] Gates sold some of his shares and received $1.6 million. His real wealth, however, was in the 45 percent of the company he still owned. The market value for his stake at that time was $350 million. Bill Gates became a multimillionaire overnight. And he was just thirty years old.

With increased stubborn determination, Gates kept building on his successes. He was not content to settle back and just be a millionaire. Gates knew he would need to stay several paces ahead of the pack to stay at the top of the software market. Microsoft continued to flood the market with new products and upgrades of existing products. Its efforts did not go unnoticed.

In April 1986, Microsoft received five awards from the Software Publishers Association. Three of the 1985 "Excellence in Software" awards were for "Best Technical Achievement," "Best User Interface," and "Best Software Product," all awards for Windows. The other two awards were "Best Business Products" and "Best Productive Product." Those awards were for Excel, a program Microsoft developed for its partnership with Apple.

Gates had such an incredible desire to win that he absolutely hated to lose.[10] He had not really ever failed at anything. Motivated by self-confidence plus a fear of falling from the top, Gates pushed Microsoft harder than ever. His strategy was for Microsoft to be the first out with an idea, and to stay in front. Their expansions into new software meant new competition. Microsoft was creating operating systems, programs, and applications software. Their products were tackling competitors of all sizes and wealth. It appeared that Microsoft was developing a monopoly on the computer software market. Several lawsuits were filed to prevent Microsoft from becoming too powerful a giant.

It is not unusual for Microsoft programmers to work eighty-hour weeks. But there's still time for fun. Bill Gates encourages his staff to work hard—and to play hard, too. Microsoft employees can take their competitive spirit onto the basketball court or the softball diamond.

Wall Street, on the other hand, was more interested in Gates's continued success. By March of 1987, the price of Microsoft stock had climbed to $90.75 a share, with no end in sight. With his 45 percent ownership of the company, Gates watched his wealth multiply. Only thirty-one years old, Bill Gates became a billionaire. He is the youngest American ever to achieve that distinction.

Five years after it went public, Microsoft stock had risen an incredible 1,200 percent. It hit record highs. The public had a new interest in technology stocks, and Microsoft was leading the way. By the end of 1991, Microsoft was worth an estimated $21.9 billion. It became the first company in business history to produce three billionaires—Bill Gates, Paul Allen, and a key executive, Steve Ballmer. Gates, however, was not interested in stock prices. His target was software and computer technology, and that was where he focused. The squeaky-voiced mathematics whiz kid had seen his dreams come to life.

Windows to
the World

In the 1980s, Microsoft had several opportunities to work with IBM in the development of the personal computer. The first was on an IBM computer called the PC/AT. "AT" stood for Advanced Technology. The PC/AT was powered with the Intel 80286 (or 286) chip, and ran on MS-DOS 3.0. IBM used its best-selling typewriter, the IBM Selectric, as the model for the computer's design.

Several IBM products were not well received by the buying public. The company shine lost some of its luster. Management at IBM knew they needed a notable product to bring them back up. They banked on the success of the PC/AT.

Although Bill Gates was committed to working

Bill Gates, age thirty-one, became a billionaire in 1987. The price of Microsoft stock was skyrocketing as the company continued to flood the market with new products.

with IBM, he did not share their devotion to the 286 chip. He knew Intel was developing a more powerful 80386 (or 386) chip. Gates tried to get IBM to change its plans. He believed the next generation of computers would be built around the 386. His vision of the future fell on deaf ears. IBM stayed with the 286 chip. This would prove to be a major disaster for IBM.[1]

IBM needed a new operating system and they again called on Gates. Microsoft went to work on IBM's OS/2. IBM had dreams of OS/2 becoming the leader in operating systems.

IBM's plan was to have one broad operating system. It was supposed to be designed to take the place of DOS. IBM wanted it to be capable of connecting all kinds of computers, from small PCs to huge mainframes.

IBM had the right idea, but not the right hardware to support it. Unfortunately, the company did not take into account the limited power of the 286 chip. IBM had invested too much to turn back.

IBM struck a new deal. They wanted Microsoft to write two operating system programs: one to run on the 286 chip, and another for the 386. IBM wanted to license from Microsoft the version of Windows that was designed to run on the 386 chip. They changed the name to Presentation Manager. IBM also wanted some changes in the software. This caused a conflict between the two companies.[2]

IBM told Microsoft to adapt the GUI to include special features used on IBM mainframe computers. Although Gates agreed to the challenge, he knew this would mean problems: Making the requested changes would be limiting to Microsoft. The new Windows version for the IBM OS/2 would not be compatible with Microsoft Windows for DOS.

Although he did dedicate a strong team to work on IBM's projects, Gates still maintained a team to develop Windows. He needed to protect himself and Microsoft in case OS/2 was not a hit. IBM, however, regarded Windows as a direct threat to the success of OS/2. The two companies battled over their different visions.

In 1987 IBM presented OS/2 with the 286 chip on its new line of PS/2 computers at an industry trade show. "PS" stood for Personal Systems. Many people who got through the crowds to see the new machines were excited by what they saw. Other leaders of the industry were not as impressed. They doubted DOS users would easily dump an operating system that already worked just to have IBM's new version. When asked, Gates praised OS/2. Insiders knew, though, that Microsoft was going ahead with the development of Windows.

IBM's OS/2 was not the success the company had hoped for. One problem was the price. OS/2 cost more than twice as much as Microsoft DOS. Hardware upgrades were necessary for people who currently had a PC. That meant spending about another $2,000 just to run the system. Even if they were willing to make the investment, few applications (programs that handle specific tasks such as word processing) were available for use with OS/2. Large corporations frowned on paying so much for a system with limited functions. Upgrades alone could cost millions of dollars. As far as computer users were concerned, Microsoft had already supplied them with all they needed. They stayed loyal to DOS.

By 1988, Windows 2.0 for DOS was introduced. It was designed to work with the powerful 386 chip. Although its debut was successful, Gates was already moving on to his next target. He had a team of programmers developing an advanced version of the operating system, called Windows 3.0. Gates had the backing of several software developers for both products. They were writing applications for Windows 2.0. They would be poised and ready to make changes when the new Windows was released.

Gates's persuasive tactics to find support for Windows presented a problem to the team at IBM. They wanted Microsoft to concentrate its energies and efforts on OS/2.

Gates pushed ahead on Windows 3.0. It was created to run "on top of" MS-DOS. That meant that the user could open programs in DOS or Windows. It was not compatible with OS/2. Gates realized he was risking the partnership with the powerful IBM. Still, if it were successful, Windows 3.0 could be the best idea he had ever developed. Gates was gambling his personal reputation and the entire fate of Microsoft.

The public liked what it saw in Windows. Gates's vision of making every computer as easy to operate as a Macintosh was what the users wanted.

Not everyone was thrilled for Bill Gates, however. The team at Apple had a problem on their hands. If computer users could purchase an inexpensive IBM clone and run it with Windows, there would be little need for Macintosh. The Macintosh line was more

At computer trade shows like this PC Expo, manufacturers and software developers show off their new products.

expensive by about a thousand dollars. Apple was losing market share. The company had to take action. In March 1988, Bill Gates and the executives at Microsoft learned they were being sued by Apple.

In a long statement that was released to the press before Microsoft heard about the lawsuit, Apple stated its case. Apple said Microsoft infringed on its design and accused Gates of using Apple's copyrighted system. Apple felt that it owned the "look and feel" of the visual display features used on the Macintosh.

The suit had a direct effect on IBM, too. Microsoft had developed Presentation Manager from Windows 1.0. Although Apple agreed to give Microsoft limited use of its system for creating Windows 1.0, use for the following version was not included.

The suit brought by Apple rocked the computer industry. Software is constantly being revised and upgraded. If Apple were to win the suit, it could stop other software companies from developing products as well.

Gates felt that Apple did not have exclusive rights to the graphic operating system. Neither Apple nor Microsoft had actually created it. The system was developed by Xerox PARC.[3] Gates also argued that there were differences between Windows and the Macintosh. Windows displays menus and files by name. Macintosh shows icons.

Other companies were awaiting the outcome of the suit. There was confusion surrounding the future of projects in the works for IBM. Leaders in the applications software industry were developing products to run with OS/2: Lotus was working on a new spreadsheet program, and WordPerfect had word processing. On August 24, 1993, the suit was finally settled.[4] After over five years of litigation, Microsoft triumphed over Apple.

It was not the first lawsuit against Gates, nor the last. The Federal Trade Commission (FTC) and the Department of Justice were also investigating Microsoft. Questions were raised about whether Microsoft had created unfair trade practice or violated any antitrust laws. Both groups stayed poised for attack for many years.

Competitors complained of a Microsoft monopoly. They believed Gates was using his operating system to give an unfair advantage to Microsoft applications software. Gates's competitors wanted the government to look into it. The FTC investigated but did not find anything conclusive. At one point, Microsoft was asked to change its licensing policies.[5] The issue was resolved for the time being.

Through it all, Gates stood his ground. His company quickly became a major player in the applications software business. Microsoft succeeded in stopping the growth of IBM's OS/2 market share, and kept the look of Windows.

On May 22, 1990, Microsoft announced the immediate availability of Windows 3.0. Gates spared no expense. The program made its debut at a glitzy, one-day, $3 million party. There were media hookups around the world for journalists, industry experts, and other software companies to witness it. The employees at Microsoft back in Seattle watched via satellite. Gates planned a media blitz, including appearances on TV talk shows. He had the support of noted software companies, such as Lotus Development Corporation. Lotus was the creator of the very popular spreadsheet program called 1-2-3. Lotus eventually agreed to develop a version for Windows.

The entire country was now familiar with Bill Gates and Windows 3.0. Consumers and businesses bought Windows, and Microsoft stock. Just one year after its introduction, Windows 3.0 was available in twelve languages in twenty-four countries worldwide.[6] Gates saw his concept of a user-friendly operating system on every computer come to life. The world applauded his efforts. There was now a GUI with multitasking (working with more than one application at a time) and with many new applications being developed. The feeling in the business was that "Microsoft is on a path to continue dominating everything in desktop computing when it comes to software. No one can touch them or slow them down."[7]

As a leader, Bill Gates has been able to keep his employees excited about their progress even through the lawsuits. He is extremely selective about whom he brings into his company. He works hard to keep the team lean. Gates believes there are "two levers in our business—head count and advertising. Advertising expense you can change very easily, and if you make a mistake, it's easy to correct. With head count you have to be more conservative. Once you allow managers to think it takes 100 people to do something when it should be 20, that's extremely hard to reverse."[8] At Microsoft, there could be just one person

Bill Gates meets famous people in every field, from business to politics to entertainment. Gates is as much of a celebrity in the business world as Steven Spielberg (right) is in Hollywood.

designated for a project that the competition might assign to twenty.

Gates has made the transition from entrepreneur to commander in chief. He manages to keep a small-business atmosphere. He is able to break down business goals into small targets that independent business units can handle. These units of marketing managers and programmers have informal meetings. Gates likes to attend them so he can voice his own ideas. "No doubt the company would do well without me at this point, but I like to think the Microsoft clock runs faster because of me."[9]

The public's perception of Bill Gates has changed several times over the years. In the early days, he was viewed as a nerdy entrepreneur. His boyish appearance was deceiving. A few years later, he was known as a software guru, and a leader for the new technology. The third wave of identity likened him to a barracuda. Gates is known for being intensely aggressive. He has made enemies with a couple of industry powerhouses. At the top of the list, most likely, is IBM. None of this seems to bother the king of the information age.

Life As a Billionaire

B_y 1996, Bill Gates was worth an estimated $18 billion.[1] His fortune became larger than his friend Warren Buffett's. Buffett is the chairman of Berkshire-Hathaway, a multibillion-dollar clothing and investment company.

Despite the lawsuits and product delays, Microsoft continued to grow and prosper. Microsoft's operating system software was found on eight out of ten of the world's personal computers.[2] Microsoft was responsible for "booting up" (starting) and running millions of machines. Bill Gates and his team also created a wide range of applications programs. Products such as Word, for word processing, and Excel, for spreadsheets, became strong leaders in their product categories. Microsoft's electronic encyclopedia, called *Encarta,* "outsells the *Encyclopedia Britannica.*"[3] Microsoft's revenue for 1994 was almost $5 billion.[4] That equaled more than the total sales of every other software maker combined. All this helped to make Bill Gates a very wealthy man. In fact, he had become the world's richest, according to *Forbes* magazine.[5]

Life as a billionaire can be exciting, but Gates is often low-key. He is sometimes considered eccentric. Although he could buy his own airline, he frequently flies coach on business trips. He is known to eat simple lunches like pizza or canned spaghetti. His dress is still casual. Of course, there are things Gates now has that his billions have provided.

For example, in the mid-1990s, Gates built an expensive lakefront mansion. The estimated cost to design and construct the house to his unique specifications was $50 million.[6] It is located in Medina, Washington, near Microsoft headquarters.

The palace-like home has forty thousand square feet of space. There is an underwater stereo system for the swimming pool. There are video "walls" that display various collections of electronic art. In addition to his famous rocking, Gates likes to jump. His new home has room for that, too. One area has a twenty-five-foot vaulted ceiling to house his trampoline. There is a thirty-car garage to accommodate any vehicle. Even the landscaping is fantastic, complete with a trout stream.

The mansion is also home to an unusual collection of souvenirs. One such piece is a clay statue that Gates brought back from China. The nine-foot-tall

Billionaires can build fabulous homes. Gates's palace, shown here under construction, has forty thousand square feet of space. Video "walls" offer a changing display of artworks.

clay replica of a warrior was unearthed twenty years ago near the city of Xian.

Bill Gates has invested in more than just his home. He has always expressed an interest in art. In November 1994, he paid $30.8 million for a special notebook.[7] It was known as the Codex Hammer. (A codex is an important manuscript.) The Codex Hammer, seventy-two pages long, contains Leonardo da Vinci's theories on water, astronomy, and geology. It includes pictures and details of his thoughts from the years 1506 to 1510. Within the Codex, da Vinci predicted the invention of the steam engine and the submarine.

Gates purchased the notebook by giving the winning bid at an auction. He later found out he was bidding against his friend Warren Buffett. Gates changed the name to the Codex Leicester, after the Earl of Leicester. The Earl had bought the Codex in 1717. It was called the Codex Leicester for 263 years. Then businessman Armand Hammer purchased it in 1980. He renamed the notebook after himself. Gates decided to break with tradition and chose not to name it the Codex Gates.[8]

Gates is an avid reader. Before he bought the famous manuscript, he read everything he could on da Vinci. He even read a translation of the Codex itself.

Gates's interest in art did not stop with the purchase of the Codex Hammer. With his own money, he opened a company called Corbis. The company's goal is to put the art and images of the world into a digital archive. Some are being placed on CD-ROMS for easy use. The idea of art archives is not new, but digital archives are. Corbis Corporation has been directly competing with other archives that sell images on a per-copy basis. Such archives include ImageBank, owned by Kodak, and PressLink, based in Virginia. Another archive, the Bettmann Archive, has an enormous file of 16 million images. In October 1995, Corbis owned about five hundred thousand images. Later that month, Gates made his move. He bought the Bettmann Archive. That was good news for computer users. Soon, the world's largest photo collections would be accessible through a modem connection. Browsing through images of everything from early America to European travel would be possible.

Bill Gates's personal life was changing, too. On New Year's Day in 1994, Bill Gates married Melinda French. She was a twenty-nine-year-old Microsoft executive from the marketing department. Gates was thirty-eight years old. The couple met at a company picnic in 1987. They were married on the Hawaiian island of Lanai in a very private ceremony. Gates spent more than $1 million on the wedding. French wore a $10,000 designer gown. There were four billionaires present that day. Warren Buffet and Paul Allen attended. Microsoft vice president and longtime friend Steve Ballmer was the best man.

Many of Microsoft's competitors hoped his marriage would slow down the aggressive Gates. The Gateses appear to have a solid relationship. "Bill's finding out that there's life outside Microsoft," said Vern Raburn, a former Microsoft executive. "And

In 1994, Bill Gates married Melinda French, an executive in the Microsoft marketing department. Here Melinda sits with her father-in-law, William Gates, Jr., a retired attorney.

having kids will deepen that process. There won't be a better father in the world," predicted Raburn in 1994.[9]

Gates was soon given a chance to discover what kind of father he would be. Bill and Melinda Gates became the proud parents of a baby girl, Jennifer Katherine, born on April 26, 1996.

Although he rarely, if ever, takes a vacation, Bill Gates has taken some exotic trips. For his fortieth birthday, in October 1995, he went on a two-week trek through China with his wife, his father, and Warren Buffett. Gates studied Chinese history and art while there. He and his group took a train ride along the Yangtze River. At one point, he and Buffett were playing bridge so "intensely that fellow passengers had to interrupt the pair" to point out the beautiful scenery.[10]

The year 1995 was also significant for Bill Gates for another reason. It was the twentieth anniversary of Microsoft. There were now over 16,350 employees.[11] Gates chose to mark the milestone quietly. He allowed brief one-on-one interviews with local reporters in his office.

Annual parties are thrown for his friends and family every July. With the excitement of a child, he picks and plans a different theme each year. He and family members play the judges as his guests play games for prizes. One year he had six tons of sand trucked in to see who could build the best sand castle.[12] About one hundred people attend each year. The party-goers end the day by writing and singing a rap song.

For the employees at Microsoft, Gates holds an

annual party to keep morale high. One year, ten thousand Microsofties attended a picnic at a private park. Gates also throws an annual Christmas gala. One of the more lavish parties was held at the new Washington State Convention Center in 1990. The floors were transformed into the common sights and landmarks of New York City. Gates enjoys the spirit and festive atmosphere.

There are many other places Bill Gates likes to put his money. In addition to investments, new businesses, and entertainment, Gates gives a great deal to charity. Many of the groups that benefit from donations are education related. He donated $12 million to the University of Washington for bioengineering research. He also gave $10 million for a University of Washington endowment. It was created in his mother's name. Another $6 million went to Stanford University for a computer science center. Gates also gives $1 million to the United Way each year.[13]

Gates eventually wants to "give away 90 percent of his fortune, partly to spare his future family the trials of managing vast wealth."[14] He is often criticized for not spreading around more of his fortune. Although he believes strongly in charitable activities, it "requires attention and 'bandwidth' that would be better devoted to Microsoft," says Gates.[15] ("Bandwidth" here refers to mental energy.)

Bill Gates has slowly let the public see another side of him. He enjoys all kinds of games, from pick-up basketball to trivia games. He also likes golf and movies. He has a tireless curiosity about everything.

Bill Gates is known among his friends as someone who likes to have fun.

Gates had a unique opportunity to show his humorous side in a TV commercial that aired only once during a Microsoft "infomercial." The ad aired in August 1995. Microsoft had a media blitz to announce a new product, Windows 95. The people at Coca-Cola thought the ad would be a good vehicle for Gates to have some fun. The story line of the ad was perfect. While working late one night, the richest man in the world suddenly realizes he doesn't have pocket change to buy a Coke. "Machines," Mr. Gates sighs, then walks back down the hall saying, "Hello? Anybody got some change for a Coke? I'll pay you back . . ."[16] With billions of dollars to his name, Bill Gates is good for the loan.

The Future Is Here

On November 27, 1995, host David Letterman had a special guest on CBS's *Late Show*. Bill Gates was promoting his new book, *The Road Ahead*. The book comes complete with an interactive CD-ROM that also plays as a compact disk.

The Road Ahead tells of Gates's vision for the future. He believes we are entering the age of information. The computer will be used for education, business, and entertainment. The advanced technology team at Microsoft has already started working on some wild ideas that one day may be reality. Some are called "hardwear." They are computing and communications devices that can be worn or carried. One is a portable pocket computer to track documents and files. There are also prototypes of running shoes with a computer in the heel. The shoe computer can clock speed, distance, and calories burned. Bill Gates likes the idea of a "wallet PC." It could work as an electronic version of everything found in a wallet or purse.

Gates sees wonderful devices coming for everyday use. Possibly, there could be one central control for all home appliances.

Microsoft has introduced many new, revised, and upgraded products over the years. Gates has taken a business that was fun for a hobby and turned it into a $100 billion industry. He is trying to stay focused on keeping Microsoft the leader. Whether a product is a success or failure, Gates keeps pushing its limits. It keeps the consumers and his competitors on their toes.

Gates worries constantly that another upstart company could do exactly what Microsoft did to the market. It keeps him restless. "If you slow down even a little bit . . . someone else can come in and take the lead."[1] As one of his vice presidents says, he believes that "no matter how good your product, you are only eighteen months away from failure."[2]

Gates looks for new growth opportunities for the software giant. One area is the Internet. The Internet was designed for government use over twenty years ago. It is a communications system that links computers through a modem. Users call using it "going online."

The Information Superhighway could hold the next biggest place for business. It is a chance to explore new territory. Gates sees the Information

As CEO of Microsoft, Bill Gates is often called upon to speak in public. In Gates's vision for the future, the computer will be essential in business, education, and entertainment—and Microsoft will continue to lead the way.

Superhighway as "the first exciting new opportunity since the invention of the personal computer."[3] Gates views positioning his business on the Internet as taking part in a gold rush.[4] There are many popular online services now available to the general public. America Online, Prodigy, and CompuServe are just a few.

Until the 1990s, Microsoft had no part in that form of the computing business. Then Gates took a closer look. Customers were paying fees to get information on their computers, and Microsoft was not getting a dime. After being sure there was a market for it, Gates decided to enter the online services business.

The introduction of this product needed a hook. His strategy was to bundle the new online service, called Microsoft Network (MSN), with the newest, upgraded operating system, Windows 95. At the time, Windows 95 was the most recent version of the original Windows 1.0. It had enhanced graphics and was designed to be easier to use. By combining MSN and Windows 95, Gates could have access to millions of potential online customers.

It had taken three years to develop Windows 95, which has 26 million lines of code.[5] Microsoft hired four hundred thousand outside testers to preview the new product.

As is standard procedure at Microsoft, Windows 95 was repeatedly delayed getting to the market. Each time, the press got a bit more information. The hype paid off in sales, but there were still many bugs that needed to be worked out.

Gates originally planned for Microsoft Network to be a basic online service. He soon shifted to make it usable for the Internet as well. Everyday transactions such as paying bills or browsing through an electronic catalog were possible through the network. Gates wanted a fee each time it was used.

Windows 95 was created to replace MS-DOS and Windows 3.1. Since the program had built-in Internet access, several online companies complained they were being pushed out because their online systems weren't automatically accessible. Once again, Bill Gates found himself in the middle of a court battle.

The Department of Justice was called again. The charges were that the software giant was practicing unfair competition. By putting Microsoft Network into an operating system that would obviously be widely used, the online services believed they were being shut out. Since Microsoft's systems control the majority of PCs, the other services could be overlooked.

There was a catch to the suit. If the Justice Department delayed the release of Windows 95, that could create trouble, too. Many other computer companies had created products to support Windows 95. New upgrades were waiting to hit the street. Even the stock market could be affected. If the Justice Department was going to stop the inclusion of Microsoft Network, it had to act quickly. The August 24 release date was rapidly approaching.

Gates decided to respond quickly. Microsoft asked a judge to block the Justice Department's probe. Its team of lawyers stated that the Justice Department had no case.

Gates pushed ahead in his position. In early July of 1995, Microsoft sent out the final version of Windows 95 to its manufacturers. Production and distribution had started. Gates beat the Department of Justice to the punch. On July 22, 1995, the Justice Department dropped its investigation.[6] Windows 95, with Microsoft Network included, made its dazzling debut as planned.

A worldwide media attack costing almost $200 million brought Windows 95 into our lives.[7] On August 24, 1995, the Corporate Campus played host to an announcement party for people in the computer trade. The atmosphere was like a carnival. There were mimes, jugglers, and clowns performing for the massive crowd. Tents were set up for software and hardware companies to display their products. In the main tent were several thousand photographers and reporters from around the globe. With comedian Jay Leno as host, Bill Gates introduced Windows 95 with a smile.[8]

Then came the public launch. A television campaign was created to reach the world. Microsoft licensed the Rolling Stones' song "Start Me Up" for use in the ad. Gates reportedly paid them $4 million to use the song.[9] There was also a report that Gates had first approached REM, the alternative rock band. He wanted to use their song "It's the End of the World As We Know It." The band members of REM were not interested.

Bill Gates had been working on other ideas, too. By forming strategic partnerships with other

To launch his Windows 95 software, Bill Gates spent almost $200 million on a media blitz. Gates would like to see Microsoft Corporation products installed on every home computer.

companies, his visions could come to life. Intuit Corporation was a potential target.

Intuit had produced a program called "Quicken." It was the best-selling software for personal finances. There were 6 million Quicken customers. In October 1994, Microsoft had announced it was prepared to pay a huge sum to acquire Intuit. Microsoft offered $1.5 billion.[10]

It appeared that a new electronic money system for handling all personal finances would be possible. The company that owned the system could charge fees. Most banks today already charge fees for use of their automated tellers.

Many members of the banking industry felt threatened. They believed that the proposed team of the software giant and the leading financial software maker could put a serious dent in their business. Gates referred to banks as "dinosaurs."[11] Once again, an antitrust lawsuit was brought against Microsoft.

By May 1995, Gates dropped his plan to buy Intuit. The lawsuit was dragging on too long. Always the aggressor, he spied another opportunity and moved on.

Microsoft announced an alliance with Chemical Bank in July 1995. Chemical was brought in to strengthen the personal money management part of Windows 95. The new team was targeting the home-banking market. Chemical's new service includes "Microsoft Money for Windows 95."[12] At this point, Gates already had agreements with six other banks as well.

Banking online was not his only objective. Later

that year, Gates announced another business arrangement. This time, the king of technology chose to link up with the National Broadcasting Company (NBC). The joint venture would produce CD-ROM software, additional online news services, and, possibly, interactive television programs. In 1996, they launched an all-news-and-business-format channel for cable television called MSNBC. Gates believed that by combining the talents of Microsoft and NBC, they would "be able to do some very unique and new things."[13] The possibility of online coverage of the Olympics or election news had arrived.

Most of Microsoft's success has been in the personal computer market. As the leader in PC software, its market value for 1995 was $46.5 billion.[14] That is almost five times as much as its nearest competitor, Computer Associates International (CA), based in Islandia, New York. That company's market value in 1995 was almost $10 billion.[15] It had success where Microsoft did not. CA is a software leader in computer network management. CA's programs are written for mainframe, midrange, and workstation computers. One of their best programs is 9 Unicenter. It helps manage computer networks.

Back at Microsoft headquarters, a new operating system was being developed. It was called Windows NT and was designed to work with a network. Gates looked for a way to boost his share of the networking business. Windows NT was a corporate version of Windows designed to control the basic functions of a network.

Gates approached Charles Wang, the chairman of

Computer Associates. The two agreed to link software companies to develop new products. They worked together for two years, and a licensing and marketing agreement was finally announced. In April 1995, they unveiled their joint production. Microsoft's Windows NT and Computer Associates' Unicenter would be offered together as one package. The potential customers were millions of corporate computer managers.

This unique package represented a major change in attitude for Gates. It was the first time another company's software was permitted to be shipped with a Microsoft product. Although both companies were already incredibly powerful and wealthy, the joint program was still very important. It meant strong growth for each.

Bill Gates has also invested heavily in new technology. His company put $35 million into Metricom, Inc., and Mobile Telecommunication Technologies

Microsoft's competitor, Computer Associates International, dominates the market for software that manages computer networks.

Corporation.[16] Gates's interest was in developing data-communications technology for handheld devices.

The consumer software division of Microsoft has been working toward new products for home use. They have been preparing multimedia "edutainment" CD-ROM disks. In 1994, they had signed a deal with Scholastic Corporation, a publisher of educational products, to codevelop new products for a younger market.

At the fall 1995 Comdex computer trade show in Las Vegas, Bill Gates was a keynote speaker. A crowd of over seven thousand packed in to hear his vision of the future. The theme of his talk was "The Office of the Future, Moving Applications to the Next Level." It was supported with a slick, Hollywood-style multimedia presentation. He spoke about workers sharing information for specific jobs. He called it "intraneting." Others simply call it networking. He also talked about developing more voice-command tools. Some voice-recognition functions are currently available. Tasks such as printing or saving on the computer can be done by voice. Gates envisions much more. He sees the possibility of checking other people's schedules or making appointments with voice command. Other tasks now being handled by a mouse or on the keyboard could soon be done this way. A voice/data modem is a part of this future. Faster processors and high-quality three-dimensional graphics are just a couple of the elements needed to make this vision of the future happen.

Charles Wang, chairman of Computer Associates, sits in the company Data Center. Wang and Gates joined forces to market two of their products—Microsoft's Windows NT and Computer Associates' Unicenter network management program.

The future of computer technology is still unfolding. Users will benefit from access to an incredible pool of information. They can explore foreign places and learn an enormous number of facts.

William H. Gates III has come a long way from the days at the Lakeside School. From a primitive piece of computer hardware, he built a multibillion-dollar industry. His incredible drive and passion have changed the way we think about computers. His use of spectacular marketing over the years has propelled Microsoft into mainstream America. Although he is feared by some and praised by others, Gates has never lost sight of his goals. Bill Gates's towering ambitions can help people work with computers when they want, where they want.

Chronology

1955—Bill Gates is born on October 28.

1971—Runs Traf-O-Data Company with Paul Allen.

1972—Works as a summer page in Washington, D.C.

1973—Briefly leaves senior year at Lakeside to work at TRW; graduates from Lakeside High School; enters Harvard University.

1975—Writes his first software program, a version of BASIC, with Paul Allen; forms Microsoft in partnership with Paul Allen.

1977—Drops out of Harvard.

1979—Microsoft moves to Bellevue, Washington.

1980—Microsoft and IBM become business partners.

1981—MS-DOS is released.

1983—Paul Allen resigns; Microsoft Windows is announced; Word for MS-DOS is introduced.

1985—Microsoft celebrates tenth anniversary with annual sales of $140 million; Gates celebrates his thirtieth birthday.

1986—Microsoft moves to the Corporate Campus in Redmond, Washington; Microsoft goes public and Gates becomes a multimillionaire overnight.

1987—Company stock hits record highs; Gates becomes the country's youngest billionaire.

1988—Windows 2.0 introduced.

1990—Windows 3.0 is released; Gates gives keynote address and his vision of the future ("Information at Your Fingertips") at fall 1990 Comdex computer trade show.

1993—Word becomes the most popular word processing program with more than 10 million users worldwide.

1994—Marries Melinda French.

1995—Microsoft celebrates twentieth anniversary; Gates presents the keynote speech ("The Office of the Future, Moving Applications to the Next Level") at the fall 1995 Comdex; Gates celebrates his fortieth birthday; *The Road Ahead* is published.

1996—Daughter Jennifer Katherine is born on April 26.

Glossary

applications—Programs that handle specific tasks such as word processing.

bugs—Glitches in software that cause problems.

CPU—Central processing unit; a computer chip that processes or reads information.

edutainment—A term for products that are educational and entertaining.

end user—An individual using a computer.

endowment—A gift of money or income.

GUI ("gooey")—Graphic user interface, an operating system in which the computer user simply clicks on an icon to perform a task.

mainframe—The largest type of computer, used to handle huge jobs.

multitasking—Opening more than one application at a time.

nondisclosure agreement—A confidential contract where both parties agree to secrecy.

operating system—A program that instructs the computer how to run.

Chapter Notes

Chapter 1

1. Nick Sullivan, "Bill-ionaire of the Year," *Home Office Computing*, January 1992, p. 76.

2. Graham Button, "The Superrich," *Forbes*, July 15, 1996, p. 124.

3. Based on the 1995 base salary of $200,000, per the New York Public Library.

4. Brent Schlender, "What Bill Gates Really Wants," *Fortune*, January 16, 1995, p. 46.

5. Tom Brokaw, *Tycoon*, NBC-TV, May 26, 1995.

6. Brent Schlender, "How Bill Gates Keeps the Magic Going," *Fortune*, June 18, 1990, p. 84.

7. Ibid.

8. Schlender, "What Bill Gates Really Wants," p. 35.

9. Janice Castro, "Is Bill Gates Getting Too Powerful?" *Time*, April 4, 1994, p. 67.

10. Brokaw.

11. Richard Brandt and Amy Cortese, "Bill Gates: The Next Generation," *Business Week*, June 27, 1994, p. 60.

12. Ibid., p. 57.

Chapter 2

1. John Seabrook, "E-Mail from Bill," *The New Yorker*, January 10, 1994, p. 51.

2. Ibid.

3. Stephen Manes and Paul Andrews, *Gates: How Microsoft's Mogul Reinvented an Industry—and Made Himself the Richest Man in America.* (New York: Simon & Schuster, 1994), p. 16.

4. Robert X. Cringley, *Triumph of the Nerds*, PBS-TV.

Chapter 3

1. Brent Schlender, "What Bill Gates Really Wants," *Fortune*, January 16, 1995, p. 40.

2. James Wallace and Jim Erickson, *Hard Drive: Bill Gates and the Making of the Microsoft Empire* (New York: HarperCollins, 1992), p. 21.

3. Aaron Boyd, *Smart Money: The Story of Bill Gates* (Greensboro, N.C.: Morgan Reynolds Publishers, 1995), p. 20.

4. Richard Brandt, "The Billion Dollar Whiz Kid," *Business Week*, April 13, 1987, p. 70.

5. Boyd, p. 28.

6. Brandt, p. 70.

7. Wallace and Erickson, p. 26.

8. Brandt, p. 70.

9. Ed Zuckerman, "William Gates III," *People*, August 20, 1990, p. 96.

10. Boyd, p. 34.

11. Ibid., p. 32.

12. Wallace and Erickson, p. 50.

Chapter 4

1. Brent Schlender, "What Bill Gates Really Wants," *Fortune*, January 16, 1995, p. 40.

2. Carrie Tuhy, "Turning Risk into Riches: Software's Old Man Is 30," *Money*, July 1986, p. 54.

3. Ed Zuckerman, "William Gates III," *People*, August 20, 1990, p. 96.

4. Ibid.

5. Stephen Manes and Paul Andrews, *Gates: How Microsoft's Mogul Reinvented an Industry—and Made Himself the Richest Man in America.* (New York: Simon & Schuster, 1994), p. 63.

6. John Seabrook, "E-Mail from Bill," *The New Yorker*, January 10, 1994, p. 58.

7. *Computer Basics* (Alexandria, Va.: Time-Life Books, 1989), p. 97.

8. James Wallace and Jim Erickson, *Hard Drive: Bill Gates and the Making of the Microsoft Empire* (New York: HarperCollins, 1992), p. 73.

9. *Computer Basics*, p. 99.

10. Zuckerman, p. 96.

11. "Key Events in Microsoft History," Microsoft Press Kit, January 24, 1995.

12. Seabrook, p. 58.

13. Zuckerman, p. 96.

14. Richard Brandt, "Billion Dollar Whiz Kid," *Business Week*, April 13, 1987, p. 71.

15. Aaron Boyd, *Smart Money: The Story of Bill Gates* (Greensboro, N.C.: Morgan Reynolds Publishers, 1995), p. 45.

16. Tuhy, p. 56.

17. Manes and Andrews, p. 91.

18. Wallace and Erickson, p. 119.

19. "Microsoft Fast Facts Reference," Microsoft Press Kit, January 24, 1995.

20. Ibid.

Chapter 5

1. Robert X. Cringley, *Triumph of the Nerds*, PBS-TV.

2. "Key Events in Microsoft History," Microsoft Press Kit, January 24, 1995.

3. Brent Schlender, "What Bill Gates Really Wants," *Fortune*, January 16, 1995, p. 47.

4. James Wallace and Jim Erickson, *Hard Drive: Bill Gates and the Making of the Microsoft Empire* (New York: HarperCollins, 1992), p. 195.

5. John Seabrook, "E-Mail from Bill," *The New Yorker*, January 10, 1994, p. 59.

6. Wallace and Erickson, p. 203–4

Chapter 6

1. Ed Zuckerman, "William Gates III," *People*, August 20, 1990, p. 96.

2. Timothy Egan, "The 6.5 Billion Dollar Man," *The New York Times*, October 29, 1995, p. 11.

3. "Microsoft Fast Facts Reference," Microsoft Press Kit, January 24, 1995.

4. Ibid.

5. Robert X. Cringley, *Triumph of the Nerds*, PBS-TV.

6. "Key Events in Microsoft History," Microsoft Press Kit, January 24, 1995.

7. "Microsoft Fast Facts Reference."

8. Ibid.

9. "Key Events in Microsoft History."

10. Brent Schlender, "Gates & Grove, Mr. Software & Mr. Hardware Brainstorming Computing's Future," *Fortune*, July 8, 1996, p. 44.

Chapter 7

1. Robert X. Cringley, *Triumph of the Nerds*, PBS-TV.

2. Ibid.

3. Ibid.

4. *Microsoft 1994 Annual Report*, 1994, p. 31.

5. Ibid.

6. "Key Events in Microsoft History," Microsoft Press Kit, January 24, 1995.

7. James Wallace and Jim Erickson, *Hard Drive: Bill Gates and the Making of the Microsoft Empire* (New York: HarperCollins, 1992), p. 362.

8. Brent Schlender, "How Bill Gates Keeps the Magic Going," *Fortune*, June 18, 1990, p. 86.

9. Ibid., p. 83.

Chapter 8

1. Graham Button, "The Superrich," *Forbes*, July 15, 1996, p. 124.

2. Philip Elmer-DeWitt, "Mine, All Mine," *Time*, June 5, 1995, p. 50.

3. Ibid.

4. Ibid.

5. Button, p. 125.

6. Personal interview with Dan McFadden, Morse McFadden Communications, Inc., September 12, 1995.

7. "Bill Gates Restores the Past," *The New York Times*, November 14, 1994.

8. Ibid.

9. David Ellis, "Love Bytes," *People*, January 17, 1994, p. 42.

10. Michelle Matassa Flores, "Gates On China; 20 Years of Microsoft," *The Seattle Times*, October 12, 1995, p. C1.

11. "Microsoft Fast Facts Reference," Microsoft Press Kit, January 24, 1995.

12. James Wallace and Jim Erickson, *Hard Drive: Bill Gates and the Making of the Microsoft Empire* (New York: HarperCollins, 1992), p. 417.

13. Paul Andrews, "Microsoft at 20, Bill Gates at 40: A Look Ahead—Could Bill Gates' Year Really Have Been So Bad?" *The Seattle Times*, August 14, 1995, p. A1.

14. Ibid.

15. Ibid.

16. "So Much Stock, So Little Liquidity," *The New York Times*, August 25, 1995, p. D4.

Chapter 9

1. Robert X. Cringley, *Triumph of the Nerds*, PBS-TV.

2. Philip Elmer-DeWitt, "Mine, All Mine," *Time*, June 5, 1995, p. 50.

3. Richard Brandt and Amy Cortese, "Bill Gates' Vision," *Business Week*, June 27, 1994, p. 57.

4. Diane Mermigas, "Bill Gates Mines Internet Gold," *Advertising Age*, April 1, 1996, p. 55.

5. Dan Beucke, "Microsoft's Hard Sell of New Windows 95," *Newsday* (Long Island), August 5, 1995, p. A6.

6. Dan Beucke, "Deeper Probe of Microsoft Abandoned," *Newsday* (Long Island), July 22, 1995, p. A19.

7. Gerry Khermouch, "Jagger Does Windows 95 *Start Me Up*," *Brandweek*, August 21, 1995, p. 6.

8. Cringley.

9. Joe Queenan, "Hoopla to Hooopla," *The New York Times*, August 27, 1995, sec. 3, p. 12.

10. Amy Cortese and Kelly Holland, "Bill Gates Is Rattling the Teller's Window," *Business Week*, October 31, 1994, p. 50.

11. Ibid., p. 50.

12. Thomas Hoffman, "Banks Balance Competitive Transactions," *Computerworld*, July 31, 1995, p. 41.

13. Robin Schatz, "Another Marriage of Giants," *Newsday* (Long Island), May 17, 1995, p. A39.

14. Michael Unger, "Two Giants Give Birth," *Newsday* (Long Island), April 26, 1995, p. A6.

15. *Computer Associates International 1995 Annual Report*, 1995, p. 6.

16. Richard Brandt and Amy Cortese, "Bill Gates: The Next Generation," *Business Week*, June 27, 1994, p. 60.

Further Reading

Atelsek, Jean. *All About Computers*. Emeryville, Calif.: Ziff-Davis Press, 1993.

Bernstein, Daryl. *Better Than a Lemonade Stand!: Small Business Ideas for Kids*. Hillsboro, Oreg.: Beyond Words Publications, 1992.

Boyd, Aaron. *Smart Money: The Story of Bill Gates*. Greensboro, N. C.: Morgan Reynolds Publishers, 1995.

Computer Basics. Alexandria, Va.: Time-Life Books, 1989.

Cusumano, Michael, and Richard W. Selby. *Microsoft Secrets: How the World's Most Powerful Software Company Creates Technology, Shapes Markets, and Manages People*. New York: The Free Press, distributed by Simon & Schuster, Inc., 1995.

Graham, Ian. *Computers*. New York: Gloucester Press, 1992.

Manes, Stephen, and Paul Andrews. *Gates: How Microsoft's Mogul Reinvented an Industry—and Made Himself the Richest Man in America*. New York: Doubleday & Company, Inc., 1993.

Math, Irwin. *Bits and Pieces: Understanding and Building Computer Devices*. New York: Scribner, 1984.

Schepp, Debra, and Brad Schepp. *Kidnet: The Kid's Guide to Surfing Through Cyberspace*. New York: HarperCollins Publishers, 1995.

Microsoft on the Internet: http://www.microsoft.com

Index